Your Breakup

Bestie

Heart & Smarts

First printing edition 2019.

ISBN: 978-0-578-42888-8

Introduction

Hey Bestie,

We know you are going through a breakup, and breakups can be difficult. It can hurt to let go and it can hurt to stay, but letting go is necessary when it is not a good match and if you aren't happy.

Letting go and facing your emotions may be hard sometimes, but we will be there for you along the way. We will use prompts to help you process your thoughts and feelings so you can get through your breakup and move forward. As *Your Breakup Besties* we will provide you with a space to allow you to release your emotions. Whether you have a lot to say, but don't know where to start, or don't know what to say, we are here to listen, guide, and support you. What are besties for?!

Your Besties,
Erica & Tina

Contents

How to Use *Your Breakup Bestie*

1. Write and/or draw what you are thinking or feeling.
2. Provide details, be descriptive, and don't hold back.
3. Be honest with yourself and what you've been through or are going through.
4. It's okay to skip a prompt that you believe has already been addressed or doesn't apply to you.
5. Use your plan on page 12 as needed and the coping skills on pages 83-120 when you are feeling blue, need things to do, or want to be in a better mood.
6. Use additional pages as needed. Write anywhere on the page, inside and outside of the images.
7. It's okay to miss your ex, to feel emotional, sad, angry, embarrassed, ashamed, and to cry.
8. If you don't understand the question/prompt you may use the examples as a guide, but try to not to limit your answer to the examples provided.
9. Try to complete all the activities in the book.
10. Optional: Send any of your favorite responses to us at YourBreakupBesties@gmail.com. We would love to hear from you.

What's Going On?

Self-Awareness is an important start. If you can identify where you are, how you are doing, and how you feel, you can decide what you want and how to get there.

Where Are You? What's Your Destination?

What brought you here? What emotional place are you at right now? What is your emotional destination? Where do you want to be emotionally? Write in the spaces below.

I....

Examples: I am crying, I can't let go, I'm sad, I am cyber stalking, I can't concentrate or focus, I'm not doing my work at school or at work.

Destination
I want to ....

Examples: I want to be myself again, I want to be happy, I want to stop crying, I want to move forward, I want to be over my ex.

Where am I?

How will you know when you have arrived at your destination? What are the signs/checkpoints that show you are headed in the right direction towards your destination? See the examples below, which include the signs at the road marks and the destination by the star.

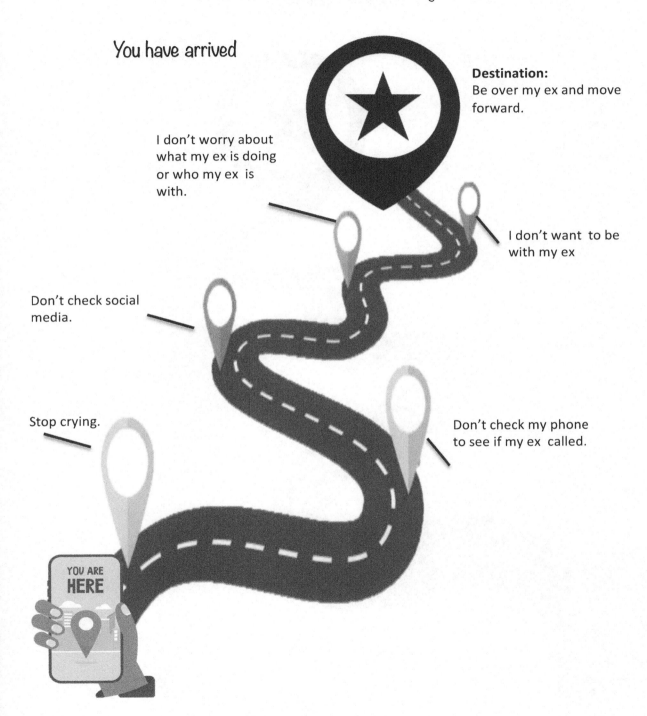

You have arrived

Destination:
Be over my ex and move forward.

I don't worry about what my ex is doing or who my ex is with.

I don't want to be with my ex

Don't check social media.

Stop crying.

Don't check my phone to see if my ex called.

YOU ARE HERE

Where am I?

Write your destination by the star (see page 8 for reference to your destination). Write the signs/checkpoints beside the road marks that let you know you are moving toward your destination. Look at page 9 for examples.

You have arrived

Destination:

Plan, Prepare, and Practice

Now that you know where you are and where you want to be, it can help to prepare and plan for the journey ahead.

Plan

Ending a relationship, even when we think it is best for us, is easier said than done, but if you are trying to stay away and move forward, it is helpful to make a plan to prepare yourself on what to do, who to talk to, or where to go when you get that urge to call, text, cyber stalk: or are feeling down.

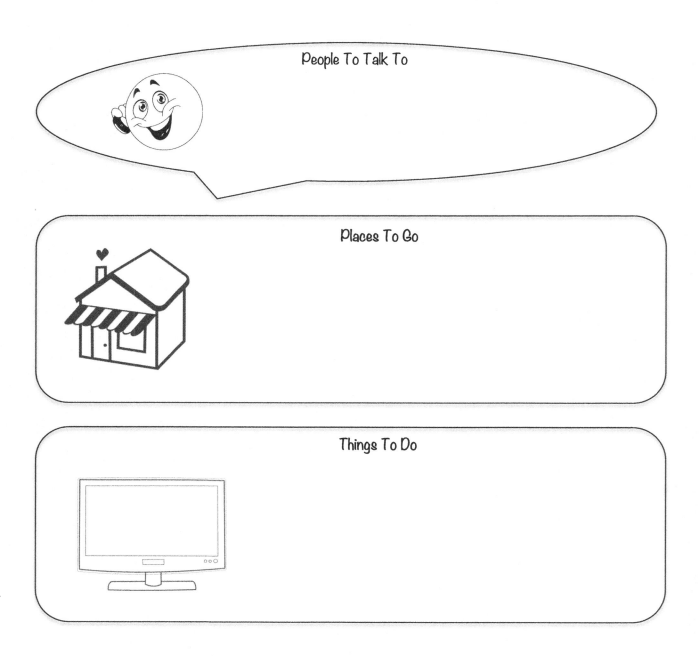

People To Talk To

Places To Go

Things To Do

Let's practice. Do one thing on your plan right now.

Prepare

People may ask you about your relationship. You may want to talk about it or you may not. You may want to say what happened or you may want to say something like "I don't want to talk about it" or "It just didn't work out." There may be some people you want to talk to and some people you don't want to talk to. It can help to prepare yourself with what you will say to people when they ask about your relationship. Write below what you will say.

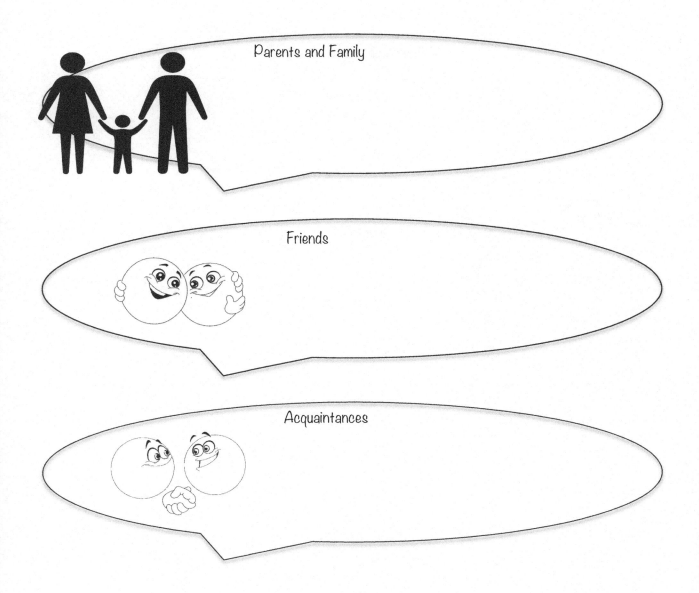

Parents and Family

Friends

Acquaintances

Practice

Your ex may say or do things to get back together with you, upset you, or to get your attention, intentionally or unintentionally. Some things may be nice, and others may not. Write below what your ex may say or do and what you will do instead of respond or get back together with your ex.

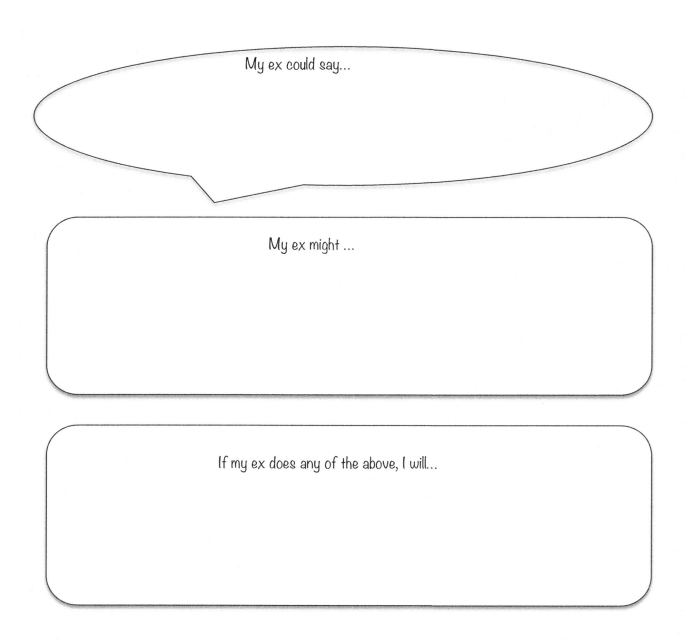

My ex could say...

My ex might ...

If my ex does any of the above, I will...

Triggers

A trigger can be a situation, event, person, place, or thing that can provoke us, set us off, leave us vulnerable, and can cause us to take a step backward from the direction we want to go in. Triggers can be harmful to the progress we make if we are not aware of them or don't plan how to respond to them. To be aware of and prepare for those provoking triggers, list your triggers below and what you can do if they occur.

Breakup Rules

If you want to move forward, let go, or start feeling better, it can help to give yourself rules to guide you and help you move forward. Write down the rules you will follow to help you get through this breakup.

Do

Don't

Examples: Do use your plan, do stay away from my ex, do call your friends, do keep yourself busy, do delete your ex from your social media accounts.	Examples: Don't be friends, don't call your ex, don't cyber stalk, don't see your ex for XX number of days.
1.	1.
2.	2.
3.	3.
4.	4.

Activity: Listen to New Rules by Du Lipa. Turn your rules into a song. Try to make it rhyme. For example, "Do use your plan and stay away as much as you can, don't call or text, don't see your ex, don't let him in your head, do leave him on read." Don't forget to sing it and dance.

What Not To Do

Before we deal with the breakup here are a few suggestions on some things you should not do.

1. Don't sit around and wait for your ex and miss out on other life opportunities.
2. Don't cancel plans you have made if your ex calls, text, or ask to see you.
3. Don't isolate yourself.
4. Don't avoid going out of the house.
5. Don't lounge around in pajama's unkempt all day, every day. Fix yourself up. If you look good you may feel good.
6. Don't post negative comments about your ex or the relationship.
7. Don't stalk your ex or show up uninvited.
8. Don't contact your ex's friends or family.
9. Don't do anything permanent until you are in a better place. For example a haircut or makeover is temporary and okay, a tattoo is permanent and you may regret it.
10. Don't cope in unhealthy ways, such as drugs, alcohol, or promiscuity.

Let It Out

It can help to release your thoughts and feelings and not hold them in. Let's begin that journey. This may be difficult so make sure you refer to your plan as needed.

What happened?
How did the relationship end?

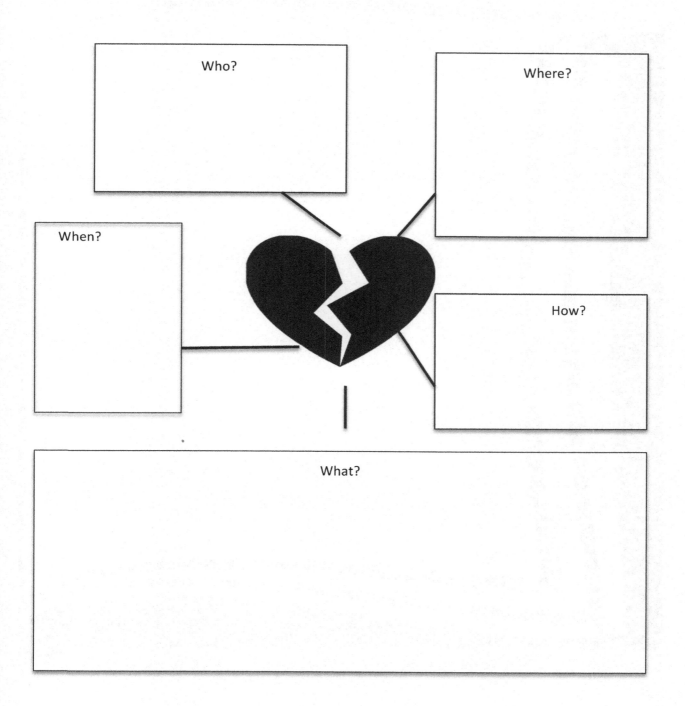

Who?

Where?

When?

How?

What?

Tell Me Everything

Tell me your story. How did you two breakup? Use these pages and the next couple of pages to describe in detail your breakup story.

Activity: Share your story with someone on your plan.

Story continued...

What's New?

Do you have an update? Return to this page and the following pages when you have an update. Go to page 30 if you don't have an update. Activity: If you are feeling down text someone from your plan.

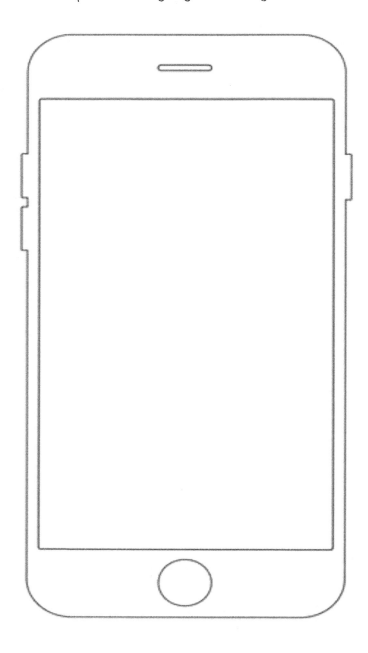

What's New?
Do you have an update? Write it below. Don't forget to text someone from your plan if you feel down.

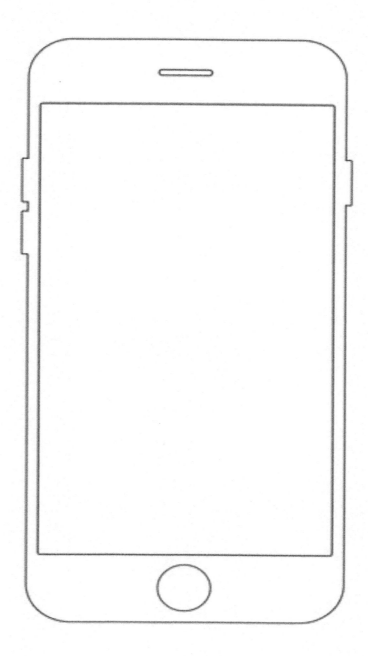

What's New?

Do you have an update? Write it below. Don't forget to text someone from your plan if you feel down.

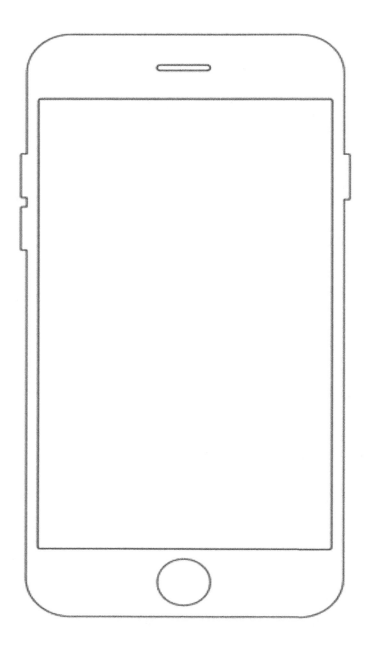

What's New?

Do you have an update? Write it below. Don't forget to text someone from your plan if you feel down.

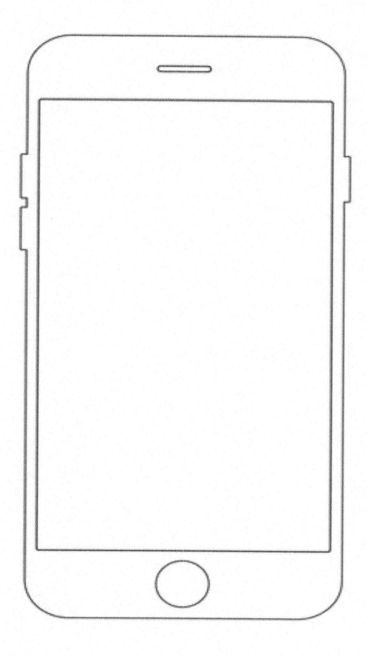

What's New?

Do you have an update? Write it below. Don't forget to text someone from your plan if you feel down.

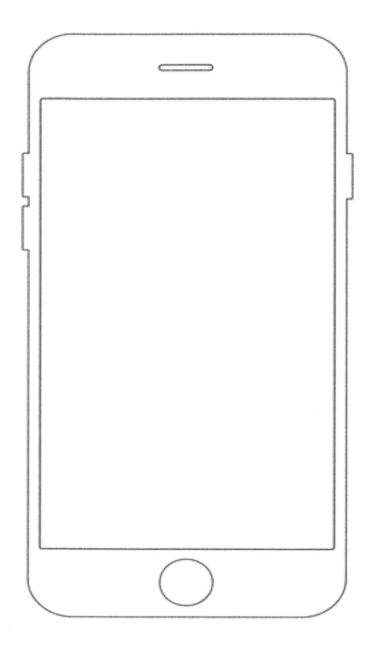

What's New?

Do you have an update? Write it below. Don't forget to text someone from your plan if you feel down.

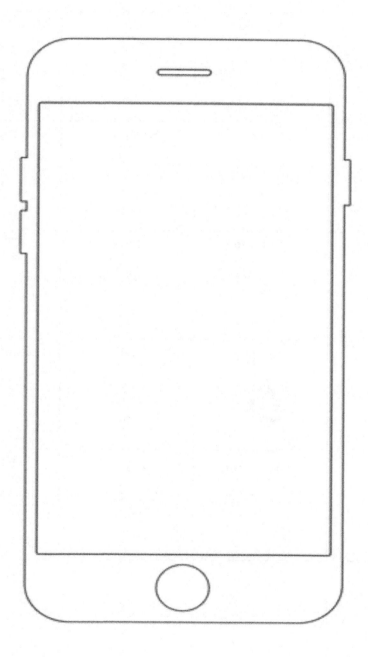

How is this <u>breakup</u> making you feel?
Circle any feelings that apply and draw any feelings not listed.

Jealous	Worried	Scared	Tired/Exhausted
Regret/ ashamed	Sick	Frustrated	Stressed
Disappointed	Confused	Sorry	"Dumb"
Annoyed	Crazy/ Insane	Sad	Embarrassed
Angry	Calm/Peaceful	Happy	Hopeful

How is this breakup making you feel?

Describe and explain your feelings on the previous page. What are your thoughts? What makes you feel that way?

Feeling sad or mad is part of the breakup and healing process so it is natural to feel sad, mad, and other feelings. If you don't like how you are feeling and want to feel differently you have to think differently. Think positive and you can feel positive. You will learn more about positive thinking later in this journal.

How did it feel to be in a relationship with your ex?
Circle any feelings that apply and draw any feelings not listed.

Jealous	Worried	Scared	Tired/Exhausted
Regret/ ashamed	Sick	Frustrated	Stressed
Disappointed	Confused	Sorry	"Dumb"
Annoyed	Crazy/ Insane	Sad	Embarrassed
Angry	Calm/Peaceful	Happy	Hopeful

How did the relationship make you feel?
Describe and explain your feelings and how often you felt like that below.

Activity: Compare these feelings with your feelings on page 30. What do you notice? Are any of the feelings the same or similar? You may remember some happy and pleasant feelings and those feelings can make you miss your ex and want to go back, but it is likely that during the relationship there were some unpleasant feelings as well. It is good to have those happy memories, but during this breakup remember there were some unpleasant feelings as well and as you feel those unpleasant feelings remember to cope and use your plan as needed.

Breakup Memes

Activity: Find or draw a picture to create a meme for the boxes below.

When you think about your ex

When you move forward

When you look back

When you realize the breakup is the best thing that could have happened to you

Breakup Memes

Activity: Find or draw a picture to create a meme for the boxes below.

When you leave your ex on read

What was I thinking?

When someone brings up your ex

When you run into your ex

Breakup Memes

Activity: Write a statement to go with the images to create a breakup meme.

Breakup Memes

Activity: Find breakup memes or create your own.

Final Words

What would you like to say to your ex? Write a letter to your ex below. Make sure you use a salutation, for example, 'Dear', 'To', 'Hey.'

You can include how your ex made you feel, what your ex did or didn't do, or anything else you didn't get to say, including goodbye.

Activity: Tear the letter into little pieces, destroy it, throw it in the trash, and get rid of it.

Let It Out

Is there something you haven't told anyone or have been holding in, perhaps because you are too embarrassed, ashamed, afraid, can't believe you were in that situation, or think no one will understand? Let it out below.

Let it out!

Let It Out

What are the reason(s) you have not talked about it? Write your reasons below. Now that you are aware and have admitted it, you can accept that it happened, and continue to the next chapter of your story.

Activity: Cut this out, tie it to a balloon, go outside and let the balloon go or write on the balloon with a marker.

SMH

Sometimes it's hard to move forward because we think about the things we did and wish we hadn't done. We shake our head with disbelief and focus on our regrets and we don't let go of them. Do you have any regrets? Let your regrets go below.

Activity: Make a list of all the god choices you have made. Remind yourself that although you may do things you regret you also make good choices, including ending this relationship.

Your Heart

Sometimes, it's hard to move forward because our heart and brain conflict. Our heart tells us one thing and our brain tells us another. What does your heart tell you?

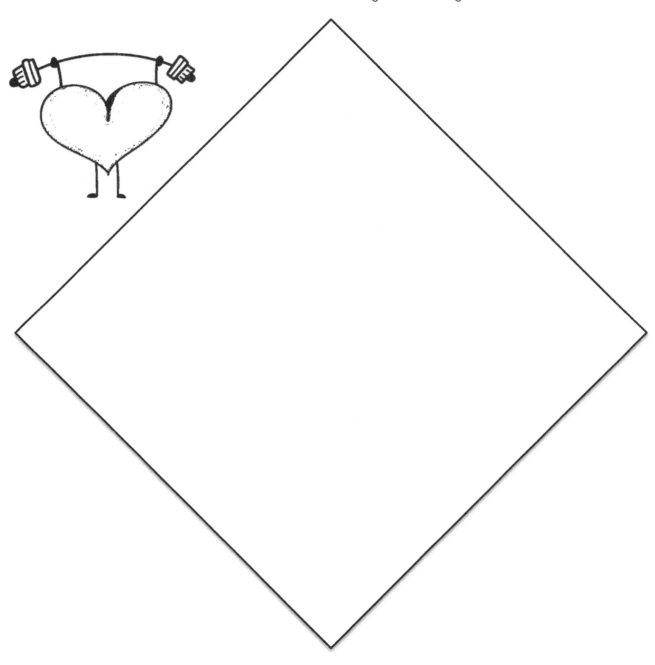

Your Brain

Sometimes, what our brain says is different from what our heart wants. What does your brain tell you? Write a letter from your brain to your heart. If your brain could talk to your heart what would it say? Make sure you start your letter by first acknowledging what your heart feels and wants. Don't forget to comfort your heart. Then allow your brain to give your heart advice and a pep talk.

Example: Dear Heart, I know you are hurting right now and you miss your ex and may want to be with your ex, but your ex is not the right person for you because...
This breakup is the right decision and you will feel better soon. You can get through this.
Love,
Your Brain

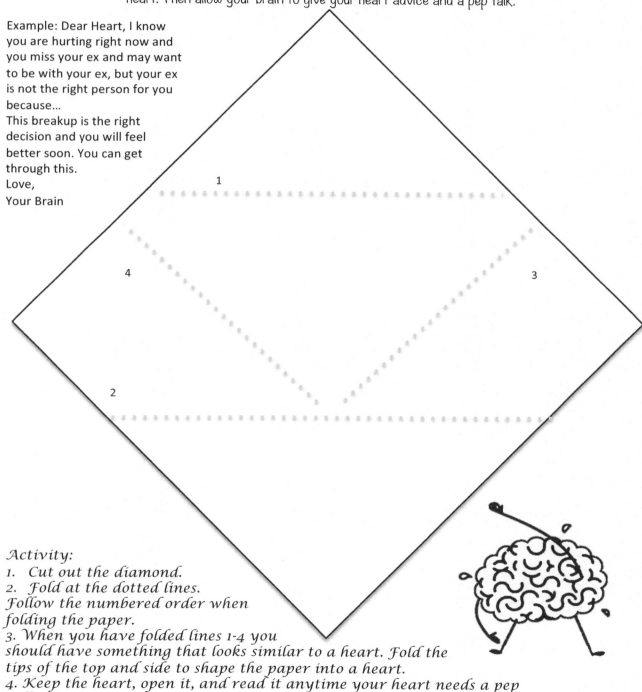

Activity:
1. *Cut out the diamond.*
2. *Fold at the dotted lines.*
Follow the numbered order when folding the paper.
3. *When you have folded lines 1-4 you should have something that looks similar to a heart. Fold the tips of the top and side to shape the paper into a heart.*
4. *Keep the heart, open it, and read it anytime your heart needs a pep talk.*

How much easier would your life be if you could just listen to your brain? How would your life look if you did?

> **Examples:** I would be less emotional and more rational, things would be easier and less complicated, I would be able to move forward, I would not blame myself, I would feel better about myself, etc.

It Ended For a Reason

It can help to let go and move forward if you remind yourself that the relationship ended for a reason.

Remind Yourself That You Broke Up for a Reason
What is the reason for your breakup? Write your reason in the heart below.

There's Usually More Than One Reason

What are the other reasons? Remember, you broke up for a reason. You cannot change someone, but you can change your situation and the choices you make moving forward. You can make choices that can help you move forward and live a happy successful life.

Activity: Look up a cupcake or cookie recipe or use a family favorite. Follow the recipe. As you crack the egg think about how the egg may have been broken, but it will become something amazing. When you think about how your heart has been broken, like the egg, bake, and remember you too are becoming more and more amazing. Make sure to share your treat.

Remind Yourself About The Things That You Don't Like About Your Ex?
What don't you like about your ex?

Remind Yourself About The Things You Didn't Like About Being In the Relationship
What didn't you like about being in a relationship?

Activity: Get a flower, take it apart one petal at a time. As you remove each petal, if the petal is big enough use a marker to write the things you don't like about your ex on each petal, or say each reason aloud, then release the petals. Feel free to take a nice big smell before you release them.

Remember What Your Friends and Family Think

What would your friends and family say about your ex, you, your relationship, or what have they said? Remind yourself of all the reasons why this breakup is what's best for you.

You deserve better.
(YDB)

Activity: Turn the helpful things they would say into text acronyms. For example, YOLO, IRL, FOMO, etc. See the example above. Repeat to yourself any acronyms that are helpful.

They Must Have Their Reasons

What are their reasons for saying that? What examples would they provide to prove what they are saying?

Remember, those who love us want to help us. You can listen to what people have to say. You don't have to take their advice, but perhaps consider if what they are saying is valid or true. An outside perspective can help you see what you are unable to see.

Remind Yourself, You Don't Want It, You Won't Have It

What don't you want in a partner? List the things you will not accept, or things you can't live with. These are often referred to as deal breakers. Check all the qualities your ex had. Remind yourself that your partner is not what you want.

Activity: Write, with a washable marker, on the back of your hand or palm of your hand, all the things you will not accept in a partner to remind yourself of why the relationship needed to end and why you will move forward.

Look at the qualities you don't accept and want. Explain why you don't want those qualities. Sometimes, we see things we don't want in a partner, yet want them to change and believe they can change. Remember, they can change only if they want to. Remember that you cannot change someone.

Activity: Write all the things you don't accept in a partner on separate sheets of paper. Crumble them into balls and shoot them in the trash as if you are playing basketball.
Activity: Clean and organize your closet, bags, and room, then decorate.

Remind Yourself, It Is Not A Good Fit

Sometimes, it's best to end a relationship because it is not a good fit. It's just not a good match. You may want different things, you may have different values, maybe your personalities don't mix well, or for whatever reason you just don't fit well together. List reasons you and your ex are not a good match. See the examples below. Write your response on the next page.

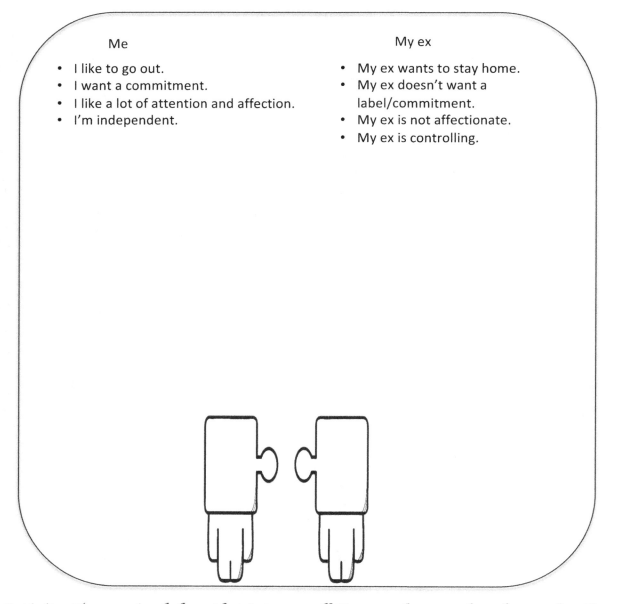

Me

- I like to go out.
- I want a commitment.
- I like a lot of attention and affection.
- I'm independent.

My ex

- My ex wants to stay home.
- My ex doesn't want a label/commitment.
- My ex is not affectionate.
- My ex is controlling.

Activity: Try a pair of shoes that is too small. You can borrow shoes from a family member or friend. As you walk around in them think about how they feel. You may be able to squeeze into them, but it is probably not comfortable and can cause some pain. Remember how important a good fit is and what can happen when you force something that doesn't fit.

Remind Yourself, You Need A Good Fit

On the left write about yourself and on the right write how your ex is not a good fit. See page 58 for examples. You may love your ex and your ex may be a good person, but your ex just may not be a good fit. Like a good pair of jeans some may be too tight, some may be too loose, and some are just the right fit and the right fit makes us feel our best.

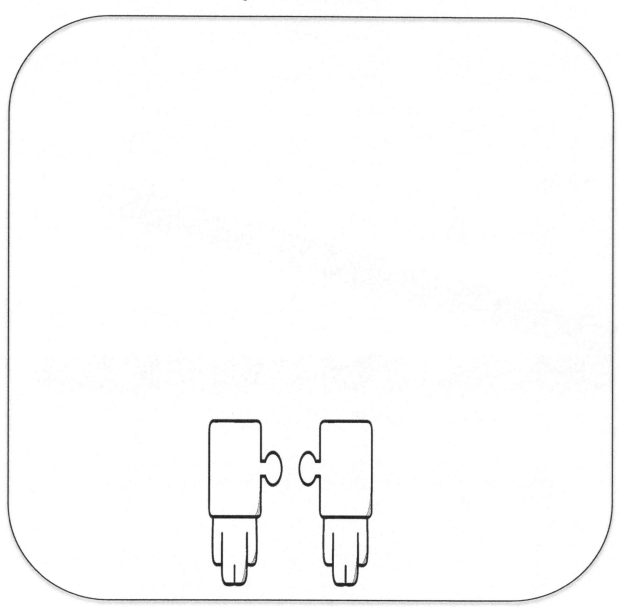

Activity: Strut in your favorite jeans today. As you strut around in them today remember how good it feels to have a great fit.

Remind Yourself that Actions Speak Louder Than Words

Sometimes, what someone says and what they do is inconsistent, but their words can leave us hopeful which can make it hard to move forward. It is helpful to see if the words you are holding on to are followed through with action. Write down in the callout images the things your ex said and in the action images what your ex did that was inconsistent with their words. See the examples then write your response on page 62-63.

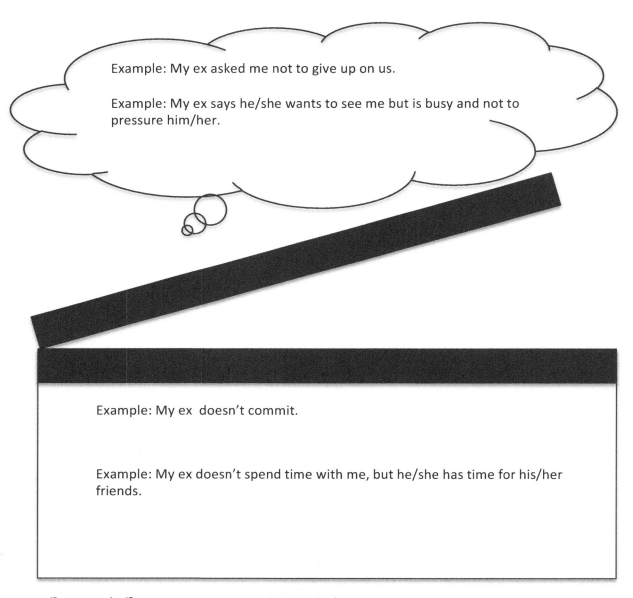

Example: My ex asked me not to give up on us.

Example: My ex says he/she wants to see me but is busy and not to pressure him/her.

Example: My ex doesn't commit.

Example: My ex doesn't spend time with me, but he/she has time for his/her friends.

For example, Do you want a partner who says he/she wants to see you or a partner who spends time with you, or both? Remind yourself that you want someone whose words and actions match.

Remind Yourself that Actions Speak Louder Than Words
Here are more examples.

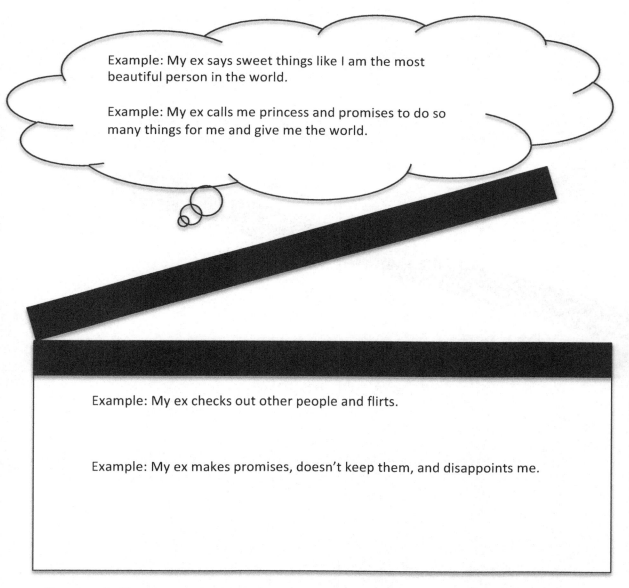

Example: My ex says sweet things like I am the most beautiful person in the world.

Example: My ex calls me princess and promises to do so many things for me and give me the world.

Example: My ex checks out other people and flirts.

Example: My ex makes promises, doesn't keep them, and disappoints me.

For example, Do you want someone who says you are beautiful or treats you like they have eyes for no one else? Do you want a partner who promises the world or gives you the world? Do you want a partner who calls you princess or treats you like one? You can want and have both. Remind yourself of any inconsistencies your ex had.

Remember, Actions Speak Louder Than Words

Write down in the callout images the things your ex said and in the action images what your ex did or didn't do did that was inconsistent with their words.

Remember, Actions Speak Louder Than Words

Write down in the callout images the things your ex said and in the action images what your ex did or didn't do did that was inconsistent with their words.

Remember Your Values

What do you value? What's important to you? Write your values then cross out the values you compromised in the relationship.

Examples: Education, friendships, religion, independence, commitment, punctuality, respect, kindness to others and myself, family, drug free lifestyle, etc.

Remember Your Values

Remember how compromising your values can affect you. Write how compromising your values affected you.

Examples: I stopped spending time with my friends, I canceled plans with others, I skipped work or school for my ex, I became dependent on my ex and stopped doing things on my own, I became mean and moody, I stopped being myself, I was embarrassed by some of the things I accepted, I hid some of the things I accepted, etc.

Activity:

1. Follow the instructions in order. Do not read the next step until you complete the step before.

2. Cut out the money below.

3. Tear it into as many pieces as you possibly can.

4. Try to tape it back together.

5. Were you able to tape it back together? How hard was it to tape it back together?

6. If this was your money would you tear your money into pieces? If you would not compromise a bill, why would you compromise your values? You are far more valuable than any bill.

Remind Yourself That The Relationship May Not Be Successful

It can be difficult to move forward when we love someone, but a successful relationship needs more than love. Write down what you need in order to have a successful relationship inside the puzzle pieces below. Color the pieces that your relationship had, take a look at the heart you colored, is your heart complete? Remind yourself of everything you need in a relationship to be successful that your relationship did not have.

Activity: Use a blank puzzle, make a puzzle, use the back of a puzzle, or cut out this puzzle and write what you need in a relationship in the puzzle pieces. Display your puzzle somewhere you can see it to remind yourself of what you need for a successful relationship.

Remember Your Ex Doesn't Have What You Want

What would you like in a partner? Make a list, then cross out the qualities your ex does not have.

Examples: Someone goal-oriented, faithful, committed, loving, affectionate, fun, and gentlemanly.

Provide details on why your ex is not what you want. Are these qualities you are willing to compromise?

Activity: Tear out any pages you have completed in this book that you want to get rid of or that have feelings you want to release. Place them in a bag or box. Find a spot to bury them. Have a little ceremony in which you say goodbye to your ex and the relationship. Make sure when you say goodbye you say all the reasons you are not together, things you don't like about your ex, how your ex doesn't meet your must have list, compromises your values, etc..

From Now On

Complete the sentences in the notes below with what you will not accept in a relationship from this point forward. Think about your responses in the previous pages to help you, such as your values, your must haves, and what you don't want. Write what you will not accept and what you deserve.

Notes

I will not accept...
Example: I will not accept someone that cheats on me.

I deserve...
I deserve to be with someone who is faithful.
I deserve to be with someone that I trust.
I deserve not to have to worry about who my ex is talking to or what my ex is doing when I am not around.

I will not accept...

I deserve...

I will not accept...

I deserve...

I will not accept...

I deserve...

I will not accept...

I deserve...

From Now On

Complete the sentences in the notes below with what you will not accept in a relationship from this point forward. Think about your responses in the previous pages to help you, such as your values, your must haves, and what you don't want. Write what you will not accept and what you deserve.

Notes

I will not accept...
Example: I will not accept someone that cheats on me.

I deserve...
I deserve to be with someone who is faithful.
I deserve to be with someone that I trust.
I deserve not to have to worry about who my ex is talking to or what my ex is doing when I am not around.

I will not accept...

I deserve...

I will not accept...

I deserve...

I will not accept...

I deserve...

I will not accept...

I deserve...

The Benefits of Moving Forward

If you want to move forward it can help to focus on the benefits of letting go and moving forward.

How Much Do You Want To Move Forward

Use the scale below to indicate how much you want to move forward. Explain your answer.

Example: A 10 I really want to move forward I don't like how this breakup is making me feel and I want to feel better. I want to be happy.

0   1   2   3   4   5   6   7   8   9   10

How Much Do You Need To Move Forward

Use the scale below to indicate how much you want to move forward. Explain your answer.

Example: A 10 it is a priority for me. There are many benefits to moving forward and many cons if I don't move forward. I don't like how I am behaving and what I am doing.

0 1 2 3 4 5 6 7 8 9 10

What Is This Breakup Causing You To Do

How is this breakup making you act/behave? Write your behavior in the action sign below. Examples: Not participating in things you used to, not hanging out with friends, taking it out on others, being negative, etc.

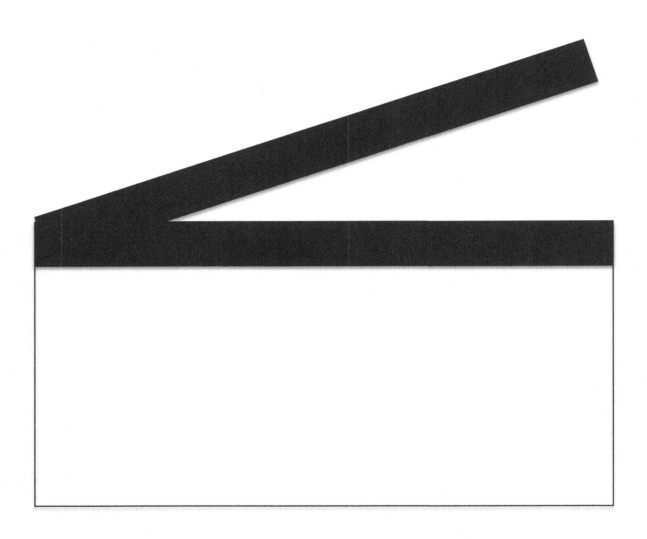

If you don't like how you are behaving or who you are becoming because of this breakup you can change it.

Are there any changes you want to make regarding your behavior?

Take Two

Our emotions can cause us to behave in unexpected ways and although we cannot control our emotions, we can control how we react to them. You have the power to control your behavior and can choose to react in a positive healthy way.

Reasons To Move Forward
What are some of the reasons you should move forward?

I am unhappy, the relationship wasn't going anywhere, it isn't a healthy relationship, I am stressed, etc.

1)_____

2)_____

3)_____

4)_____

5)_____

6)_____

7)_____

8)_____

Benefits of Moving Forward
What are the benefits of moving forward?

I will be happy, I will feel better, I will feel less stressed, there won't be anymore drama.

1)_____

2)_____

3)_____

4)_____

5)_____

6)_____

7)_____

8)_____

If You Don't Move Forward
What would your life look like now and in the future?

Use Your Coping Skills

Breakup Cycle/Pattern

If you have tried to move forward before and found yourself going back to the relationship, reflect and think if you have formed a relationship cycle or pattern? Sometimes, it is the cycle we have formed that keep us from moving forward, and you must break the cycle in order to move forward. See the example of relationship cycle below. If you have formed a relationship cycle/pattern write it on page 86-87.

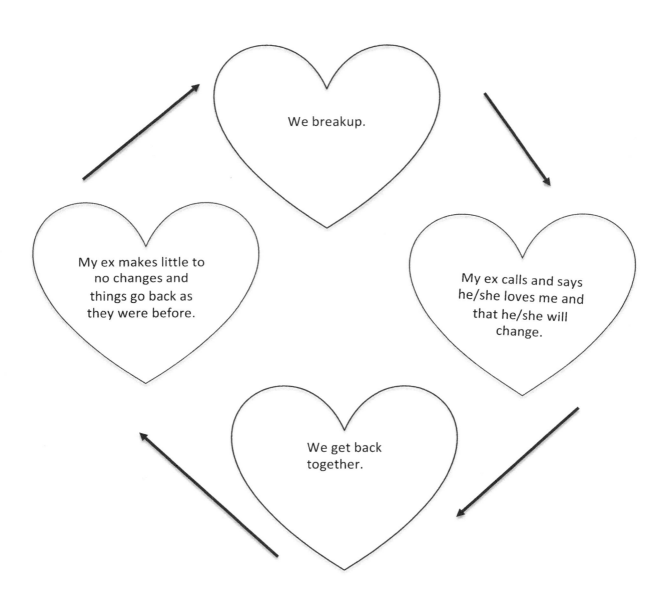

We breakup.

My ex makes little to no changes and things go back as they were before.

My ex calls and says he/she loves me and that he/she will change.

We get back together.

Break Cycle/Pattern

If you find yourself in a relationship cycle and want to move forward try breaking the cycle and forming a new cycle/pattern. See the example of a broken cycle and new pattern.

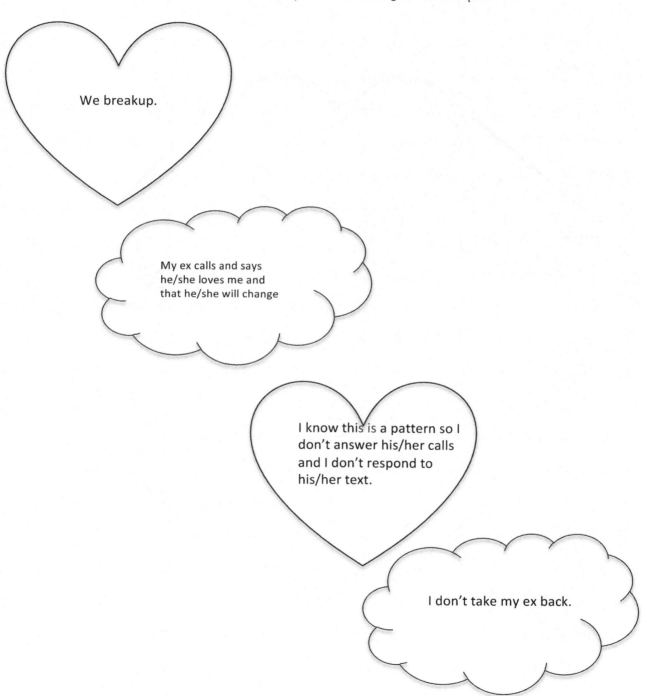

We breakup.

My ex calls and says he/she loves me and that he/she will change

I know this is a pattern so I don't answer his/her calls and I don't respond to his/her text.

I don't take my ex back.

Breakup Cycle/Pattern

If you have formed a relationship cycle write it below

Break The Cycle/Pattern

If you have formed a cycle and want to move forward break the cycle with a new pattern. Write your new pattern below.

What Does it Take to Move Forward

What do you need to do? Put what you need to do to move forward in the box below.

Examples: I need to keep busy, I need to distance myself from my ex, I need to accept that it didn't work and that's okay. I need to get rid of my ex's things, I need to change my phone number, etc.

Activity: If you are ready and have not done so, place everything that reminds you of your ex in a box and place that box out of sight, you can get rid of it, store it, or give it to someone to hold.

I'm Tough

Breakups are tough, but you're tougher. Remember how tough you are. Provide some examples of how or when you are tough. Refer to this list whenever you doubt your ability to get through this breakup.

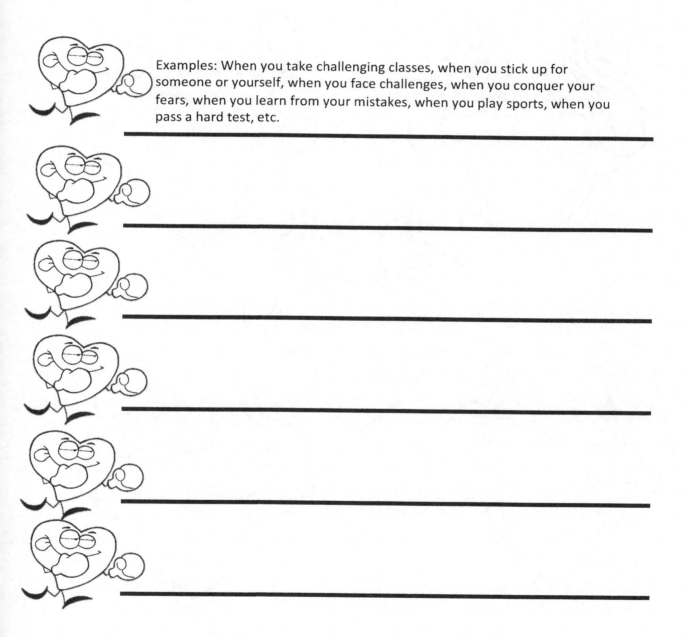

Examples: When you take challenging classes, when you stick up for someone or yourself, when you face challenges, when you conquer your fears, when you learn from your mistakes, when you play sports, when you pass a hard test, etc.

_____

_____

_____

_____

_____

_____

Your Strengths

What are your strengths and how can you use those strengths to move forward? Example: I'm helpful so I can volunteer somewhere, I'm social so I will spend time with friends and family and/or attend social events Write your response below.

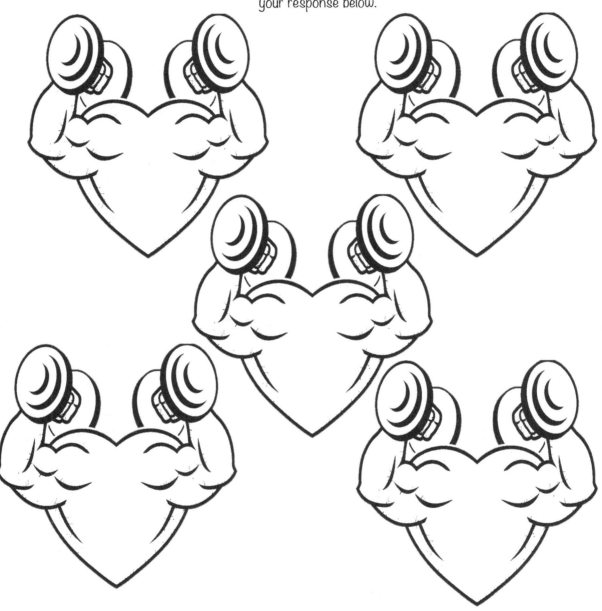

Activity: Exercise, lift weights, do push ups, yoga, Zumba, or other healthy physical activities.

Song List

Write down a list of songs that make you feel better. Listen to them when you need not only cheering up, but need to get up. Include songs that empower you or are just fun and make you want to dance. Listen to these songs whenever you are feeling down.

Activity: Create a playlist on your phone, tablet, or other device. Listen to your playlist and dance!

Keep-Busy List

Breakups can be difficult, especially when we have free time to think about the person and the relationship. It is helpful to keep yourself busy and occupied with things you enjoy or serve as distractions. Write down a list of things you enjoy and things to keep you busy.

Activity: Try & fill your planner with as many activities as possible.

I Love Me

List things you love about yourself inside and out.
Refer to this list when you are feeling down or need a reminder of how awesome you are.

*Activity: Write the things you love about yourself on pieces of paper.
Place them in a jar and take one out whenever you need a reminder of
how great you are.*

For You

Activity: Answer the questions about your best friend. Provide the next page to your friend to complete.
Share your answers with one another.

What I like most about you is...
Your biggest strength is...
What I admire about you is...
What makes you a god friend is...
The kind of partner or relationship I would like for you is...
You deserve a happy and healthy relationship because

For Your Friend

Activity: Ask your friend to complete the statements below about you. Share your answers with one another.

What I like most about you is...
Your biggest strength is...
What I admire about you is...
What makes you a god friend is...
The kind of partner or relationship I would like for you is...
You deserve a happy and healthy relationship because

Accomplishments

Although the relationship may not have been successful, instead of focusing on how the relationship failed, you can focus on your successes/accomplishments in the past, present, and future. Write your name and your accomplishments below (e.g., you will be graduating, you passed a class, you made something, you joined a sport, you learned something, or achieved a goal).

This Certificate is Awarded to:

_____

For Accomplishing:

_____

_____

_____

_____

Activity: Frame this certificate to remind yourself of all the great things you have accomplished and celebrate. Loved ones, music, and junk food is a must, a cake/cupcake is ideal.

What Would You Tell A friend?
What are some helpful things you would tell a friend or family member in your situation?

Do You Tell Yourself The Same?

Do you tell yourself the same helpful things you would tell a friend or family member? Why or why not?

Activity: Look in a mirror and tell yourself the helpful things you would tell someone else in your situation.

Good News

The breakup may be causing you to feel sad or down or maybe some mixed emotions, but don't let it keep you down. Think about the positive and good things going on in your life. Post the good things happening in your life on the social media app below and on the next page.

What's going on?

Activity: If you have good news, post it on social media, only if you think you will receive supportive and positive responses.

Chase Me

 What's going on?

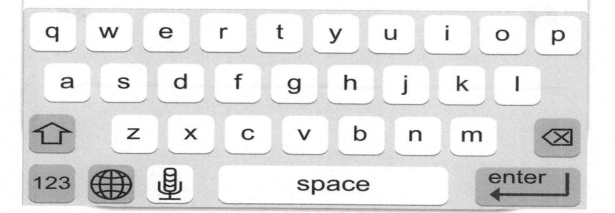

Encouraging Words

Write statements, phrases, or quotes you can repeat to yourself whenever you are feeling down and need encouragement..

"   "

_____

"   "

_____

"   "

_____

"   "

_____

Activity: Write the phrase or quote on post its and post them somewhere you can see them or set them as reminders on your phone.

#LettingGo

Activity: Turn the phrases or quotes into hashtags.

_____

_____

_____

_____

#ImLoveable, #ImAGoodCatch, #GettingStronger, #Wiser,
#MovingForward

My Loved Ones

Even though you lost your ex, instead of focusing on the loss, you can remind yourself that there are other great people in your life whom you love and care for, or who love and care for you. List the people you love and care for and vice versa, and why you love them and appreciate them.

Activity: Write them a note, card, or letter telling them how much they mean to you and how thankful you are to have them in your life.

Lessons Learned

Although you may have lost a relationship and may have some regrets, instead of focusing on what you regret focus on the things you learned. List what you gained or learned from the relationship.

Activity: Write a thank you letter for everything you learned from this experience.
Activity: Listen to Thank You Next by Ariana Grande.

You Learned So Much You Can Write a Book

Activity: Let's start with a table of contents. Write a title for each chapter you would have in your book. You can write about lessons learned, what you will do differently next time, advice you would give, etc. Write your chapter titles below. Be as clever and creative as you can be. Have fun with it.

Table of Contents

Chapter 1:

Chapter 2:   5

Chapter 3:   10

Chapter 4:   15

Chapter 5:   20

Chapter 6:   25

Chapter 7:   30

Chapter 8:   35

Chapter 9:   40

Chapter 10:   45

Your Book Cover

Activity: Every book needs a title and picture. Write your book title below.
Draw, print, or cut out from magazines the picture for your cover.
Remember to be creative and have fun.

You Can Jump Hurdles

Think of difficult times you were able to get through? What was your hurdle? Write your response below the hurdle. How did you get through those tough times? How did you jump over those hurdles? Write your response above the hurdle. If you have overcome a tough time in your life remember that you are capable of getting through this tough time as well. Use the skills you used to get through that tough time to get through this tough time.

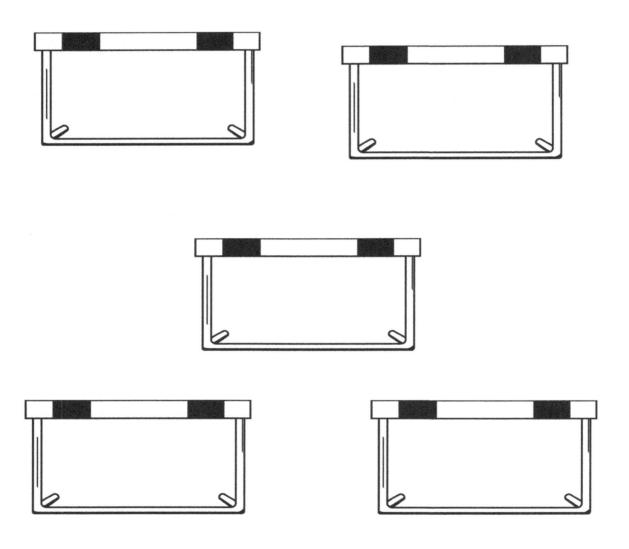

Activity: Go for a walk, jog, run, hike, or bike ride. When you are done give yourself a challenge by making the activity harder. You can make it longer or set a goal to complete the activity faster. Continue to do the activity until you meet the challenge.

Focus On The Facts

Sometimes, it is not our past that holds us back. It is thinking about the possibilities, the 'What if." If you want to move forward, you can look at the 'what is!' vs 'what if?' 'What if' is questionable and 'what is,' is factual. Write down your what-if thoughts and change them to what-is thoughts.

What If?

Example: What if we can make it work?

What is!

Example: It hasn't worked. Your ex is not trying or has tried, but it didn't work.

No More Excuses

Sometimes, it is our justifications and excuses that hold us back. Although we know what is best for us or know we should move forward, we justify our reasons to hold on and stay. If you want to move forward turn your justifications and excuses to logic and reasoning.

Justification/Excuses

- Examples: But I love my ex.
- But my ex was so good in the beginning.
- But we were together for a long time

Logic/Reasoning

- Examples: However, my ex is not a good match for me, I am not happy, and the relationship needs more than love to work.
- However, my ex is no longer good to me and I am not happy with my ex.
- However, I am not going to devote any more time to someone or something that is not working and is not making me happy.

You Have the Power, Use It

Sometimes, we give our power and control to someone else and that can leave us feeling helpless and powerless. You can get your power back by thinking about what you want and what you are choosing vs. what your ex wants and what your ex chooses. Write your helpless/powerless thoughts below and change them to power thoughts.

Helpless/Powerless Thought

Example: My ex doesn't love me

Power Thought

Example: I don't want someone who doesn't love me

Identify Your Negative Thoughts

Sometimes, it is our negative thoughts that make it difficult for us to move forward. What negative thoughts keep you from moving forward? Write your negative thoughts in the thought bubbles below.

- Examples: I can't live without my ex.
- I will never get over my ex.
- I will never find someone else.
- It's too hard.

Change Your Negative Thoughts

You can feel better and move forward if you change negative thoughts to positive thoughts. See the examples below.

- Example: I can adjust to a new life without my ex. I managed to live life without my ex before I met him/her.
- In time my feelings can fade. In time my heart can heal.
- I don't know what the future has in store for me, but I am now free to meet someone new.
- It may be hard, but it's not impossible.

You Are Loveable

Sometimes we think we weren't loved or cared for by our ex. However, that is probably not the reason the relationship ended there may be other factors. So instead of wondering if your ex loved you remind yourself of all the reasons you are loveable. Write the reasons inside the hearts below. What you have to offer may not be a good match for one person, but you have a lot to offer, and it may be the perfect match for someone else.

Examples: I'm kind, I'm faithful, I'm catering, I'm affectionate, I'm beautiful, I'm fun, etc.

Activity: Voice record all the reasons you are loveable. Have fun and be creative. You can use Animojis or social media features to record your loveable reasons. Play it over and over or anytime you need a reminder of how loveable you are.

Your Best Response, IRL

If your life was a reality TV show and your breakup episode was streaming, how would you like to see yourself respond to the breakup? How would you like the viewers to see you respond to the breakup? Write your ideal breakup episode in the TV below.

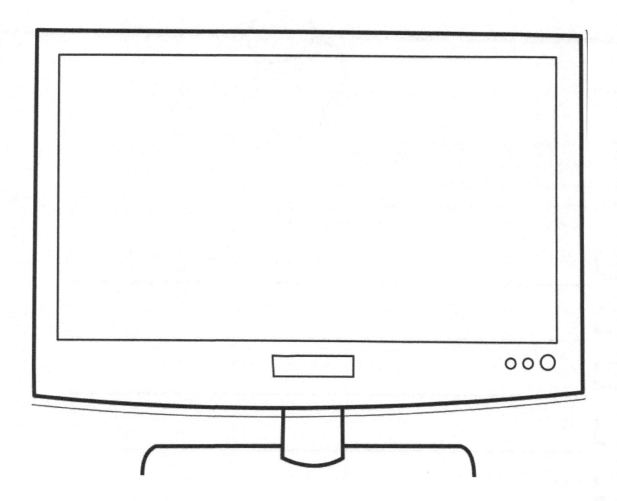

Now that you have visualized how you want to respond to this breakup you can make your ideal response real and shine like the star you are meant to be. Activity: Who is a TV character that you admire and would like to be like? Make a list of all the reasons you like that character. Highlight the qualities that you have just like that character. If there are qualities you admire that aren't highlighted and you want to adopt go for it.

Notes

What have you learned about your past relationship from *Your Breakup Bestie*. Check the boxes that apply and write in the lines below anything else you learned.

- ❑ My ex did not meet my Must Have list.
- ❑ My ex has qualities from my Won't Have It List.
- ❑ My ex is not good match.
- ❑ My ex is not consistent with my values.
- ❑ My ex was unfaithful, dishonest, controlling, or flirtatious.

❑ _____

❑ _____

❑ _____

❑ _____

❑ _____

Reminders, What Am I Really Losing?

If you find yourself feeling down about the person or relationship you lost remind yourself of the reasons why the relationship was not working, will not work, or what you are really losing. Check the boxes that apply below and write in the lines anything else you wrote in the previous page.

- ❑ I'm letting go of someone that did not meet my must have list.
- ❑ I'm letting go of someone that has qualities on my Won't have it list.
- ❑ I'm letting go of someone that is not good match.
- ❑ I'm letting go of someone that is not consistent with my values.
- ❑ I'm letting go of someone that was unfaithful, dishonest, flirtatious, or controlling.

❑ _____

❑ _____

❑ _____

❑ _____

❑ _____

Yay You!

It's important and helpful to recognize the progress you make and celebrate it.

Yay You!

What improvements have you made since the breakup? What signs do you see that show you are getting better? Write your improvements below. See the example below.

E.G. No More Cyberstalking, No More Crying, More Socializing

Keep It Up

What have you been doing to help you feel better? What will you continue to do, or what changes will you add to keep feeling better so you can move forward and get to your happy ending? Write inside the space below. Examples: I will continue to stay busy, I will continue to volunteer, I will continue to change my negative thoughts to positive thoughts.

Moving Forward

If you see signs that show you are feeling better, then it sounds like your heart is listening to your brain, and your heart and brain have made up. What will your future look like when you move forward?

How Are You Feeling Now?

Circle or draw the feelings that apply. Are you feeling better? If you are not feeling better continue to use your plan, remind yourself of how tough and wonderful you are, continue changing negative thoughts to positive thoughts, and use the other coping strategies in this book.

Jealous	Worried	Scared	Tired/Exhausted
Regret/ ashamed	Sick	Frustrated	Stressed
Disappointed	Confused	Sorry	"Dumb"
Annoyed	Crazy/ Insane	Sad	Embarrassed
Angry	Relaxed	Happy	Hopeful

Did You Reach Your Destination?

Where are you now? Refer to page 10 for your destination and checkpoints. Check off each checkpoint you reached. If you did not reach your destination, but have reached your checkpoints, continue to do what is helping you. If you have not reached your destination or checkpoints, are feeling worse or not progressing, and you think you may need professional help, please seek any professional help you think you may need.

You have arrived!

Destination:

YOU ARE HERE

Takeaways
Write anything you want to remember or that you believe is important to note.

Your Future

Your Future
Write 1-3 Goals
(Relationship, personal, or life goals)

Goal 1:

Goal 2:

Goal 3:

Next Steps

What are your next steps for accomplishing your goals and having the future you want? If you write it down, you are one step closer to achieving your goals.

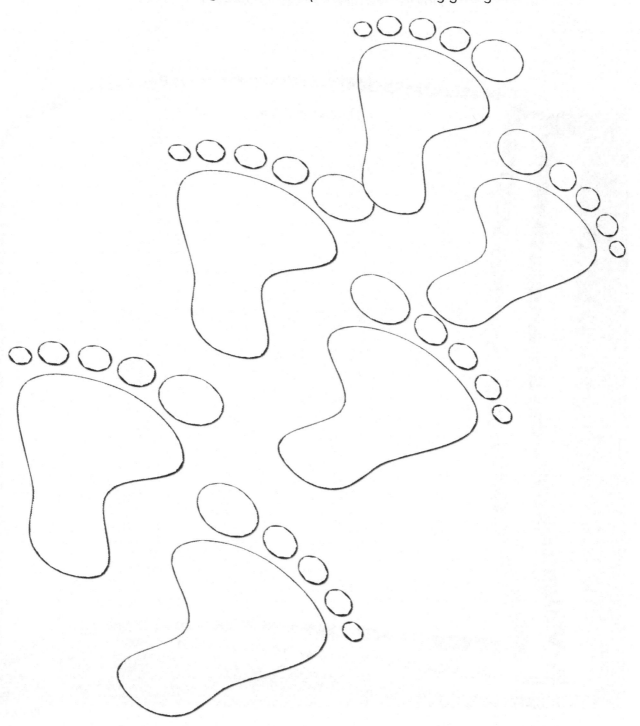

Your Happy Ending

Tell me the rest of your story. How have you moved forward, who you are now, how you have grown, and how you think your future will turn out. Write your story below and make sure you include how you became stronger, wiser and the goals you achieved.

Once upon a time...

And you moved forward, grew stronger, wiser, and happier.

You did it Bestie! You used your heart and smarts and you have become stronger. You can use your strength and the tools you learned to put your steps into action, move forward, and live your happy ending.

Your Dating
Bestie
Check or Ex?

Erica Meza, LCSW
Tina Luna

Your Dating Bestie
Check or Ex?

Dating can be complicated, when your heart says one thing and your brain another, leaving you in a grey area. Now there is a checklist to help. This journal provides prompts to help you evaluate your relationship by weighing your pros, cons, cost and benefits of the relationship. This journal reviews healthy and unhealthy relationships and much more. The journal includes scales for you to rate your relationship, and determine if the relationship is healthy and a good match for you.

Available on Amazon

Your Breakup
Bestie
Heart & Smarts

Erica Meza, LCSW
Tina Luna

Your Breakup Bestie
Heart and Smarts

Breakups are tough, but you can be tougher with the right coping skills. It can be difficult when your heart wants one thing and your brain another. This journal contains over 50 prompts and over 30 activities that incorporate pop culture, such as memes, hash tags, social media, text, and more to help you cope through a breakup. This journal will help develop coping skills that you can use to get through any other tough time in your life. *Your Breakup Bestie* is here for you. What else are Besties for?!

Available on Amazon

For more information, questions, comments, or concerns, email us at
yourbestiebooks@gmail.com

Get Your
Copies
Today

Made in the USA
Las Vegas, NV
15 April 2022

47521636R00077